1

Buffalo Bills
OFFICIAL
TRIVIA BOOK

TM / © 1989

THE
Buffalo Bills
OFFICIAL
TRIVIA BOOK

TM/© 1989

Scott Pitoniak

ST. MARTIN'S PRESS
NEW YORK

Design by Stanley S. Drate/Folio Graphics Co., Inc.

Library of Congress Catalog Card Number: 89–62669

ISBN: 0-312-03737-6

10   9   8   7   6   5

To my wife, Susan, whose support made this book possible; to my daughter, Amy, who has brought true happiness into my life; and to my mother, who got me interested in writing in the first place.

ACKNOWLEDGMENTS

The author wishes to thank the following people for their contributions to the production of this book: Ed Abramoski, Scott Berchtold, Vic Carucci, Kristen Depowski, Gary Fallesen, Larry Felser, Pete Fierle, Mike Galanti, Ted Haider, Joe Horrigan, Michael Jackowski, Denny Lynch, Milt Northrop, Bill Polian, Ken Polk, Dave Senko, George Witte, John Weibusch, and Rick Woodson. Thanks, also, to the Buffalo Bills for their help and resources.

CONTENTS

The greatest Bill of them all: O. J. Simpson. *(Buffalo Bills)*

INTRODUCTION

The story broke on October 17, 1959.

"Buffalo to Have Team in New Pro Football League Next Fall" read the headline in that day's Buffalo *Evening News*.

The announcement was greeted with plenty of skepticism by Buffalonians, who had witnessed the passing of a pro team only 10 years earlier when the old All-American Football Conference folded.

Even Ralph Wilson, the millionaire who was bringing the new American Football League franchise to town, had his doubts.

"I thought there was a one-in-ten chance of us surviving," the Bills owner admitted years later. "We were the longest of longshots."

But the Bills and the other charter members of the fledgling AFL beat the odds. They successfully challenged the NFL, forcing a merger with the established league in 1970 that revolutionized pro football.

Three decades after their formation, the Bills aren't merely surviving, they're flourishing.

In 1988 the team came within 11 points of making its first Super Bowl appearance and the fans poured out their money and their souls to establish a pro football home attendance record. It was a remarkable accomplishment, considering the Bills play in one of the NFL's smallest markets.

The support, however, wasn't surprising. After all, the Bills have become as much a part of Buffalo as spicy chicken wings and blinding blizzards.

"You'd be hard-pressed to find more enthusiastic fans anywhere in the country," said former Bills guard Conrad Dobler. "In a blue-collar area like Buffalo, where most season-ticket holders are real people as opposed to big corporations, pro football isn't merely a diversion; it's a religion."

As this love affair between town and team enters its thirtieth year, it's an ideal time to look back at some of the memorable events and colorful personalities who have contributed to the Bills' rich history.

The questions in this trivia book will test your knowledge of Bills football—and jog your memory.

Those who don't remember life before Jim Kelly may learn a thing or two. And those who bleed Bills red and blue may find some of the questions as difficult to solve as an unexpected safety blitz.

It's my hope you'll have as much fun answering these questions as I've had preparing them.

Enjoy.

—SCOTT PITONIAK
July 4, 1989

THE
Buffalo Bills
OFFICIAL
TRIVIA BOOK

Quarterback Jack Kemp guided the Bills to two AFL championships and went on to become a highly successful politician. *(Buffalo Bills)*

PRE-GAME
WARM-UPS

TM/© 1989

1   Name the two Heisman Trophy winners drafted by the Bills.
●

2   Buffalo has gone through kickers the way Elizabeth Taylor has gone through husbands. Which kicker has had the longest tour of duty with the Bills?
●

3   What Bills coach once caddied for the brother of gangster Al Capone?
●

4   In 1988 Andre Reed caught 71 passes to establish a club record for receptions in a season. Whose mark did he break?
●

5   True or false: Jack Kemp completed fewer than half of his passing attempts during his career with the Bills.
●

6   What Bill once came close to winning a National Punt, Pass and Kick competition as a nine-year-old?
   a)   Jack Kemp
   b)   John Kidd
   c)   Cornelius Bennett
   d)   Jim Kelly
●

7   Name the two men who have been with the Bills organization for all 30 seasons.
●

8   Who was the first player drafted by the Bills?
●

9   What Bills head coach once got trapped in a Rich Stadium elevator just hours before a game against the Indianapolis Colts?
●

10   Who said after the Bills' AFC East title-clinching victory in 1988: "We've just liberated Paris, but it's 600 miles to Berlin"?
●

11   What was Elbert Dubenion's nickname?
●

12 In which city was Ralph Wilson originally instructed to place his American Football League franchise?
  a) Cincinnati
  b) Louisville
  c) Miami
  d) St. Louis

●

13 How many players and draft choices did Buffalo send to Indianapolis in 1987 to acquire linebacker Cornelius Bennett?

●

14 What team did the Bills defeat in the 1964 and 1965 AFL championship games?

●

15 Jim Kelly loves to talk about his brothers. How many does he have?

●

16 Who is the Bills' second all-time leading rusher?

●

17 Name the three defenders who formed the Bills' Bermuda Triangle.

●

18 What Bill said: "Pro football gave me a good perspective when I entered the political arena. I had already been booed, cheered, cut, sold, traded, and hanged in effigy."?

●

19 What Bill attended the same Louisiana high school as Pittsburgh Steelers great Terry Bradshaw?

●

20 What was War Memorial Stadium affectionately known as?

●

21 In what round was former Bills great Tom Sestak chosen during the 1962 draft?

●

22 Name the Bill who set an NCAA Division III field goal percentage record while playing basketball for Wabash (Indiana) College.

●

23 Where did Bills General Manager Bill Polian play football in college?
   a) Manhattan College
   b) Fordham University
   c) New York University
   d) Hofstra University
   •

24 True or false: 1988 marked the first time the Bills went unbeaten at home during the regular season.
   •

25 What Baseball Hall of Famer is a cousin of O. J. Simpson's?
   •

26 Who was the Bills' first head coach?
   •

27 Which running back once carried the ball 288 consecutive times without fumbling it?
   a) Cookie Gilchrist
   b) Jim Braxton
   c) Joe Cribbs
   d) Wray Carlton
   •

28 Name the Bills assistant coach who once rushed for two touchdowns in the Super Bowl.
   •

29 From which country did Pete Gogolak and his family flee in 1956?
   a) Poland
   b) Hungary
   c) Soviet Union
   d) Romania
   •

30 Name the two quarterbacks chosen ahead of Jim Kelly in the famous 1983 draft.
   •

31 What's Cookie Gilchrist's given name?
   •

32 What all-time Bills great later became the team's general manager?
   •

GAMES TO SAVOR, GAMES TO FORGET

CARDIAC COMEBACKS

October 25, 1987. Buffalo 34, Miami 31, overtime, Joe Robbie Stadium. The Bills dropped behind 21–0, but battled back in the second half. Jim Kelly completed 18 of 23 passes for 244 yards and two touchdowns after intermission and Robb Riddick scored three touchdowns. Riddick's two fourth-quarter scores were set up by Scott Schwedes' fumbles. Scott Norwood's 27-yard field goal 4:12 into overtime were the decisive points.

October 28, 1962. Buffalo 45, Denver 38. Bears Stadium. The visiting Bills trailed 38–23 with 11:57 to go, but stormed back behind quarterback Warren Rabb. He threw touchdown passes of 75 and 40 yards, scored a two-point conversion and also ran the ball in from the four for the winning TD.

September 10, 1967. Buffalo 20, New York Jets 17. War Memorial Stadium. Buffalo scored 20 straight points in the fourth quarter, Mike Mercer, who was making his Bills debut, kicked the winning field goal.

November 22, 1981. Buffalo 20, New England 17. Rich Stadium. With only 35 seconds remaining, the Bills drove 73 yards in two plays, and won the game when Joe Ferguson's Hail Mary pass was deflected into the arms of Roland Hooks.

September 16, 1974. Buffalo 21, Oakland 20. Rich Stadium. The Bills pulled out the Monday-night victory when Joe Ferguson hit Ahmad Rashad with a 31-yard scoring pass with 26 seconds remaining.

Jim Kelly engineered one of the Bills' greatest comebacks on October 25, 1987, against Miami, when he guided Buffalo from a 21–0 deficit to a 34–31 overtime victory. *(Robert L. Smith)*

TEN LARGEST MARGINS OF VICTORY

November 1, 1970	at Boston Patriots	45–10	+35
September 18, 1966	Miami	58–24	+34
October 3, 1976	Kansas City	50–17	+33
September 13, 1981	at Baltimore	35–3	+32
October 11, 1964	at Houston	48–17	+31
December 8, 1963	New York Jets	45–14	+31
September 6, 1981	New York Jets	31–0	+31
November 6, 1966	at Miami	29–0	+29
November 20, 1960	at Los Angeles Chargers	32–3	+29
October 23, 1960	Oakland	38–9	+29
September 21, 1975	New York Jets	42–14	+28

TEN LARGEST MARGINS OF DEFEAT

October 10, 1971	Baltimore	0–43	−43
September 15, 1968	Oakland	6–48	−42
October 4, 1987	Indianapolis	6–47	−41
September 15, 1985	at New York Jets	3–42	−39
December 14, 1969	at San Diego	6–45	−39
October 30, 1977	at Seattle	17–56	−39
December 12, 1976	at Baltimore	20–58	−39
December 20, 1970	at Miami	7–45	−38
November 12, 1972	at New York Jets	3–41	−38
November 7, 1971	at Miami	0–34	−34

33 True or false: Joe Ferguson established a team record for interceptions with 25 in 1983.

●

34 When Shane Conlan led the Bills in tackles in 1987, he became the first rookie to accomplish the feat since (fill in the blank) in 1977.

●

35 In 1988, the Bills set an NFL single-season attendance record by playing in front of 622,793 fans at Rich Stadium. What team held the previous record?

●

36 What was the score of the 1964 AFL title game when Bills linebacker Mike Stratton made his famous hit on San Diego Chargers running back Keith Lincoln?

●

37 What NFL team did Ralph Wilson own stock in before forming the Bills?
a) Chicago Bears
b) Chicago Cardinals
c) Cleveland Browns
d) Detroit Lions

●

38 Who said: "A lot of business executives tell me that worker productivity on a Monday is directly related to whether the Bills lost the day before."?
a) Mayor James Griffin
b) Ralph Wilson
c) Ed Rutkowski
d) Bill Polian

●

39 Name the former Bills lineman who was the only active professional football player killed during the Vietnam War.

●

40 Who is Buffalo's all-time interception leader?
a) Steve Freeman
b) Mark Kelso
c) Butch Byrd
d) Tony Greene

●

41 This Bill caught 10 passes for 255 yards and four touchdowns in a 1979 game against the New York Jets to establish an NFL receiving yardage record for rookies. Who was he?

•

42 What Bills offensive guard gained post-football fame in a Miller Lite beer commercial?

•

43 True or false: Greg Bell gained more yardage during his rookie year with the Bills than he did during his entire college career at Notre Dame.

•

44 What coach said: "Some men enjoy rebuilding cars; I enjoy rebuilding football programs."
   a)   Marv Levy
   b)   Chuck Knox
   c)   Hank Bullough
   d)   Lou Saban

•

45 What's Cornelius Bennett's nickname?

•

46 Who was the Bills' first team captain?

•

47 What Bill posed nude for *Playgirl* magazine?

•

48 In a December 13, 1987, game in the Indianapolis Hoosier Dome, the Bills held this all-time great running back to a career-low 19 yards in 11 carries. Name the back.

•

49 Name the three Bills who have appeared in the Pro Bowl a club-record five times.

•

50 Who had a 74-yard punt return to spark the Bills' 23–0 romp over the Chargers in the 1965 AFL championship game?

1. Syracuse's Ernie Davis in 1962 and Southern California's O. J. Simpson in 1969.
2. John Leypoldt (1971–76).
3. Lou Saban.
4. Frank Lewis had 70 in 1981.
5. True. Kemp completed only 46.5 percent of his passing attempts.
6. d) Jim Kelly.
7. Owner Ralph Wilson and trainer Ed Abramoski.
8. Richie Lucas of Penn State in 1960.
9. Hank Bullough.
10. Marv Levy.
11. Golden Wheels
12. c) Miami.
13. Four. Running back Greg Bell, a first-round draft pick in both 1988 and '89, plus a second-rounder in '89.
14. San Diego Chargers.
15. Five.
16. Joe Cribbs, 4,445 yards.
17. Nose tackle Fred Smerlas and inside linebackers Jim Haslett and Shane Nelson.
18. Jack Kemp.
19. Joe Ferguson.
20. The Rockpile.
21. The seventeenth.
22. Pete Metzelaars hit 72.4 percent of his shots from the field during his career with the Little Giants.
23. c) New York University.
24. True. The Bills won all eight of their regular-season home games and also defeated Houston in a home playoff game.
25. Ernie Banks, the former Chicago Cubs first baseman.
26. Buster Ramsey.
27. c) Joe Cribbs.
28. Elijah Pitts.
29. b) Hungary.
30. John Elway by the Colts and Todd Blackledge by Kansas City.
31. Carlton Chester Gilchrist.
32. Stew Barber.

Bills kicker Pete Gogolak revolutionized pro football with his side-winding kicking style. *(Buffalo Bills)*

33. False. The record is 26 and is shared by Jack Kemp (1964 and '67) and Dennis Shaw (1971).

34. Shane Nelson.

35. Detroit Lions in 1980.

36. San Diego was leading 7–0.

37. d) Detroit Lions.

38. c) Ed Rutkowski.

39. Robert Kalsu.

40. c) Butch Byrd with 40.

41. Jerry Butler.

42. Conrad Dobler.

43. True. Bell rushed for 1,100 yards during his rookie NFL season in 1984. He had a total of 870 yards during his career at Notre Dame.

44. d) Lou Saban.

45. Biscuit.

46. Laverne Torczon.

47. Bobby Chandler.

48. Eric Dickerson.

49. O. J. Simpson, Joe DeLamielleure, and Fred Smerlas.

50. Butch Byrd.

Buster Ramsey (above) served as the first Bills head coach while Marv Levy is the team's current field boss. *(Robert L. Smith)*

FIRST
QUARTER

BUFFALO BILLS

1960 30 Years of Pro Football 1989

TM / & 1989

1   What kicker learned of his release during Coach Lou Saban's post-game radio show?
   a)   Booth Lusteg
   b)   John Leypoldt
   c)   George Jakowenko
   d)   Benny Ricardo

●

2   What Bills coach recruited Jim Kelly to play for the University of Miami?

●

3   What team did Chuck Knox leave to become coach of the Bills?

●

4   How much money did the Bills spend to acquire Jack Kemp off the waiver wire in 1962?
   a) $1
   b) $100
   c) $1,000
   d) $10,000

●

5   What Bills coach once told his team after a victory: "Well, fellows, we chalked one up in the L column."?

●

6   True or false: O. J. Simpson led the Bills in rushing in each of his nine seasons with the team.

●

7   What was Ahmad Rashad's given name?

●

8   At one point during the 1988 season, the Bills had six first-round draft choices in their starting defensive lineup. Name them.

●

9   What vocation has Fred Smerlas jokingly said he would like to pursue once his playing days are through?

●

THE MAN WHO
PAYS THE BILLS

Some things you may not have known about Bills owner Ralph Wilson:

He was born on October 17, 1918, in Columbus, Ohio. His father was a superb salesman who hit it big when he sold an insurance policy to the Chrysler Corporation in the mid-1930s. At the time it was the largest group life and health insurance policy in America. Wilson and his dad shared an interest in sports and business. They were among a group of sixty people who once owned stock in the Detroit Lions.

Wilson played freshman baseball and had an unsuccessful audition with the boxing team while at the University of Virginia. After earning his bachelor of arts degree, he attended the University of Michigan Law School, but left during World War II to join the Navy. He served aboard mine sweepers in the Mediterranean Sea and the Pacific and Atlantic oceans. He and his crew were featured in a 1944 edition of *Saturday Evening Post* magazine.

Horse racing was his first serious sports venture. Wilson recalls purchasing his first horse in 1950 for $7,000. He was elated until a trainer friend of his told him that the horse had a bum knee. But Wilson's been riding winners in the horse business ever since. Today, he owns about sixty of them, and regularly sells his breeders at the Keeneland (Kentucky) July Select Yearling Sale, the most prestigious horse auction of the year. Super-rich Sheik Mohammed al-Maktoum is one of his customers.

Wilson originally was awarded an American Football League franchise in Miami, but the city refused to give him a lease to the Orange Bowl because the previous pro football tenant had gone bankrupt and failed to meet its rent payments. The league then offered Wilson a choice of five other cities— Cincinnati, St. Louis, Louisville, Denver, and Buffalo. The would-be owner selected Buffalo, upon a recommendation from a Detroit *Times* sports editor and a superb sales job of the city by Buffalo *Evening News* Managing Editor Paul Neville.

Bills Braintrust: General Manager Bill Polian, left, and owner Ralph Wilson, right. *(Robert L. Smith)*

Financially, the Bills make up only a small part of Ralph C. Wilson Industries. The Detroit-based conglomerate consists of five television stations, an insurance agency, a concrete paving company, a tool-and-die manufacturing firm, an oil and gas drilling operation, thoroughbred horse racing, and the Bills. Wilson said the television stations are his biggest revenue producers.

10 Match the player with his college:

Joe DeLamielleure	Bluffton College
Robert James	West Virginia
Scott Norwood	Michigan State
Pete Gogolak	Fisk College
Jim Braxton	James Madison
Elbert Dubenion	Cornell

●

11 Who did the Bills trade to Pittsburgh in 1978 to acquire wide receiver Frank Lewis?

●

12 What player wore No. 32 during O. J. Simpson's first training camp with the Bills in 1969?

●

13 Which running back once sang the national anthem before a Bills home game?
a) Joe Cribbs
b) Anthony Steels
c) Lionel Vital
d) Speedy Neal

●

14 True or false: Scott Norwood's educated toe was the difference in nine of the Bills' 12 victories in 1988.

●

15 What do O. J. Simpson, Paul Maguire, and Ahmad Rashad have in common besides having played for the Bills?

●

16 Who did Cookie Gilchrist call "Little Cookie"?

●

17 What's the significance of the date October 17, 1959?

●

18 Five Bills players went on to become NFL head coaches. Name them.

●

19 Why did Bills fans rip down the goal posts at Rich Stadium following a 17–7 victory against the Miami Dolphins in the 1980 season opener?

●

20 What player did the Bills acquire from the Boston Patriots in what's believed to be the first trade in AFL history in 1960?
a) Cookie Gilchrist
b) Butch Byrd
c) Elbert Dubenion
d) Wray Carlton

●

21 According to long-time Bills trainer Ed Abramoski, this eccentric player used to chew on Coke bottles, eat worms, and do hook slides into the goal posts after scoring touchdowns in practice.
a) Tom Rychlec
b) Cookie Gilchrist
c) Glenn Bass
d) Ernie Warlick

●

22 Who said after Jim Kelly signed his five-year, $8.5 million contract with the Bills: "It takes a lot of money to buy a Rembrandt."
a) A. J. Faign
b) Bill Polian
c) Ralph Wilson
d) Hank Bullough

●

23 True or false: Jeff Wright set a Bills rookie sack record when he recorded five of them during the 1988 season.

●

24 What was Buster Ramsey's real first name?

●

25 Name the starting linebackers during the Bills championship years in the mid-1960s.

●

26 What coach labeled Cornelius Bennett the next Lawrence Taylor?

●

27 Marv Levy owns a master's degree from Harvard University. What is it in?

●

28 During O. J. Simpson's 2,003-yard season in 1973, three teams held him under 100 yards. Name them.

●

29 What two players hold the Bills record for the longest kickoff return—102 yards?
a) Keith Moody and Curtis Brown
b) Keith Moody and O. J. Simpson
c) Curtis Brown and Charley Warner
d) Charley Warner and Ed Rutkowski

●

30 Who intercepted a pass with 10 seconds remaining to preserve a 31–27 wildcard playoff win against the New York Jets on December 27, 1981?

●

31 True or false: Thurman Thomas, Cookie Gilchrist, and Booker Moore each wore No. 34 with the Bills.

●

32 Who did the Bills receive in the trade that sent Daryle Lamonica to the Oakland Raiders?

●

33 In the 1988 draft the Bills used their first pick to choose running back Thurman Thomas. It was the fourth time in club history the Bills used their first selection on an Oklahoma State player. Name the three other early Okie State selections.

●

34 True or false: 1961 Heisman Trophy winner Ernie Davis signed with the Cleveland Browns despite receiving a larger contract offer from the Bills.

●

35 What former Bill once served as Erie County Executive?

●

36 What NFL team originally selected Mark Kelso in the 10th round of the 1985 draft?
a) Chicago Bears
b) New York Giants
c) Philadelphia Eagles
d) New England Patriots

●

37 What former Bill went on to become assistant athletic director at Penn State?

●

38 True or false: The Bills were the first team to bid for Jack Kemp when the Los Angeles Chargers placed him on waivers.

●

39 Who had more sacks in his rookie NFL season: Cornelius Bennett or Lawrence Taylor?

●

40 Who was Billy Shaw referring to when he said: "We knew he was scared to death when he went under the guard for the snap."?
   a)   Jack Kemp
   b)   Daryle Lamonica
   c)   Dennis Shaw
   d)   Richie Lucas

●

41 Name the quarterback who was a backup on the Bills 1980 AFC East championship team and who also played for Buffalo's replacement team during the 1987 players' strike.

●

42 How many times did O. J. Simpson lead the NFL in rushing?

●

43 Name the two NFL stadiums with larger seating capacities than 80,290-seat Rich Stadium.

●

44 What Pittsburgh Steeler Hall of Famer does Ralph Wilson often compare Bruce Smith to?

●

45 What running back took O. J. Simpson's place after the Juice was dealt to San Francisco in 1978?

●

46 What Bills center was notorious for holding penalties?

●

47 Who coached the Boston Patriots to a 38–7 exhibition victory over the Bills in the first AFL game ever played?

●

48 Match the player with his alma mater:

Leonard Smith	Notre Dame
Jack Kemp	Nebraska
Art Still	Central Michigan
Walt Patulski	McNeese State
Ron McDole	Occidental College
Ray Bentley	Kentucky

●

49 What NFL team did Pete Gogolak leave the Bills for?

●

50 Heading into the 1989 season, this player held the record for most games played with the Bills.

a) Joe Devlin
b) Fred Smerles
c) Joe Ferguson
d) Steve Freeman

Paul Maguire before he became a television star. *(Buffalo Bills)*

1. b) John Leypoldt
2. Lou Saban
3. Los Angeles Rams
4. b) $100.
5. Hank Bullough
6. True.
7. Bobby Moore.
8. Bruce Smith, Art Still, Shane Conlan, Cornelius Bennett, Leonard Smith, and Derrick Burroughs.
9. Professional wrestling.
10. Joe DeLamielleure, Michigan State; Robert James, Fisk College; Scott Norwood, James Madison; Pete Gogolak, Cornell; Jim Braxton, West Virginia; Elbert Dubenion, Bluffton College.
11. Paul Seymour.
12. Gary McDermott.
13. b) Anthony Steels
14. False. Norwood's kicking provided the decisive points in six Bills wins.
15. Each went on to become a network football analyst.
16. Ed Rutkowski.
17. That was the date Ralph Wilson went public with his intentions of establishing an American Football League team in Buffalo.
18. Tom Flores (Los Angeles Raiders); Kay Stephenson (Bills); Lindy Infante (Green Bay Packers); Marty Schottenheimer (Cleveland Browns and Kansas City Chiefs); Sam Wyche (Cincinnati Bengals).
19. They were ecstatic because the Bills had snapped an NFL record 20-game series losing streak.
20. d) Wray Carlton.
21. a) Tom Rychlec.
22. a) A. J. Faign.
23. False. Bruce Smith had 6.5 during his rookie season in 1985.
24. Garrard.
25. Harry Jacobs, Mike Stratton, and John Tracey.
26. Former Alabama coach Ray Perkins.
27. English history.
28. Miami held the Juice to 55 yards on October 21; New

Orleans limited him to 79 on November 4; and Cincinnati slowed him to 99 on November 11.

29. c) Curtis Brown and Charley Warner.

30. Bill Simpson.

31. True.

32. Tom Flores and Art Powell.

33. Reuben Gant, 1974; Phil Dokes, 1977; Terry Miller, 1978.

34. True. Davis reportedly took less money so he could team with Jimmy Brown in the more-established NFL. But his wish never came true because he died of leukemia in 1963.

35. Ed Rutkowski.

36. c) Philadelphia Eagles.

37. Richie Lucas.

38. False. Buffalo actually put in the second bid behind Denver, but the Bills were awarded his rights by then AFL commissioner Joe Foss.

39. Taylor had 9.5 to Bennett's 8.5, but Bennett played in eight fewer games than L.T.

40. a) Jack Kemp.

41. Dan Manucci.

42. Four. 1972–73 and 1975–76.

43. Los Angeles Memorial Coliseum (92,516) and the Pontiac (Michigan) Silverdome (80,638).

44. Mean Joe Greene.

45. Roland Hooks.

46. Will Grant.

47. Lou Saban.

48. Leonard Smith, McNeese State; Jack Kemp, Occidental College; Art Still, Kentucky; Walt Patulski, Notre Dame; Ron McDole, Nebraska; Ray Bentley, Central Michigan.

49. New York Giants.

50. d) Steve Freeman.

SECOND
QUARTER

1 What quarterback did Lou Saban reportedly stuff into a locker because he refused to run a play the coach had sent in?
   a) Daryle Lamonica
   b) Jack Kemp
   c) Dennis Shaw
   d) Ed Rutkowski

●

2 Who was Fred Smerlas describing when he said: "He came in on a spaceship with a ray gun. He's a very odd man."?
   a) Jamie Mueller
   b) Art Still
   c) Ronnie Harmon
   d) Scott Norwood

●

3 True or false: Jack Kemp was sacked an NFL-record 11 times during a 1967 game against the Oakland Raiders.

●

4 What former Bills receiver won a silver medal in the long jump at the 1960 Summer Olympics in Rome?
   a) Glenn Bass
   b) Elbert Dubenion
   c) Bo Roberson
   d) Ernie Warlick

●

5 In which film did O. J. Simpson make his movie acting debut?
   a) *The Towering Inferno*
   b) *Goldie and the Boxer*
   c) *Killer Force*
   d) *Firepower*

●

6 True or false: The Bills are the only franchise in the AFC East not to have made an appearance in the Super Bowl.

●

7 Name the members of the Electric Company offensive line that paved O. J. Simpson's way to a 2,003-yard rushing season in 1973.

●

Joe Ferguson owns most of the Bills career passing records. *(Buffalo Bills)*

8 According to Bills trainer Ed Abramoski, this linebacker lived in his car outside War Memorial Stadium during the 1965 season.

●

9 Name the baseball owner who once served as an assistant on Lou Saban's staff at Northwestern University.

●

10 This punter set an NFL record when he pinned 33 of his kicks inside the opposition's 20-yard line one season.
   a) Paul Maguire
   b) Billy Atkins
   c) Marv Bateman
   d) John Kidd

●

11 The Bills finished the 1988 season with five starters who began their careers in the United States Football League. Name them.

●

12 True or false: Scott Norwood has never kicked a field goal of 50 or more yards during an NFL regular-season game.

●

13 Who caught a 35-yard Hail Mary pass as time expired to give the Bills a dramatic 21–17 win over the New England Patriots in a 1981 game?
   a) Joe Cribbs
   b) Roland Hooks
   c) Jerry Butler
   d) Frank Lewis

●

14 What Bills linebacker was named after a good-hearted gunfighter played by Alan Ladd in a 1950s movie?

●

15 Who kicked the winning field goal in Buffalo's 38–35 overtime victory against the Miami Dolphins in 1983, giving the Bills their first win in the Orange Bowl in 17 years?

●

16 Name the two members of the Bills Silver Anniversary team who went on to become NFL scouts.

●

ABE'S FLAKES

Ed Abramoski became the Bills trainer shortly after the team's arrival in Buffalo in 1960. Thirty years, ten head coaches, and 2,000 players later, Abe still is taping ankles, doling out advice and telling stories. His favorite tales are about the crazy characters who have contributed to the Bills' colorful history. Here's a look at some of Abe's favorite flakes:

Cookie Gilchrist. Like Ralph Kramden, this burly running back always seemed to be involved in some get-rich-quick scheme. He once purchased land in Canada because he was told it contained a gold mine. "Turns out, there wasn't any gold mine; there wasn't even any property," recalls Abe. "The guy had sold him a bogus deed for some property that actually was sitting at the bottom of one of Canada's deepest lakes." Cookie later ran his own maid service in Toronto. ("Lookie, lookie, here comes Cookie" read the advertising slogan on the side of his van.) It soon went out of business. He also tried to make a buck selling ear muffs bearing the Bills logo before Buffalo's 1964 championship game. But the Canadian resident failed to get a permit to bring the merchandise across the border, and he was left holding the bag again.

Tom Rychlec. He played three seasons with the Bills, leading the club in receiving in 1960 with 44 catches for 581 yards. But his pass-catching talents were overshadowed by his idiosyncrasies. "He was one strange dude," says Abe. "He would chew on Coke bottles and eat worms. But the thing he was best known for was his hookslides. He'd run out onto the field, do hookslides into the goal posts and signal either 'out' or 'safe' like a baseball umpire."

Henry Schmidt. He played only one year with the Bills, but that was long enough to earn him a spot on Abe's All-Flake squad. According to Abe, Schmidt lived in his car outside War Memorial Stadium during the 1965 season. "Guys didn't make much money playing ball in those days, so Schmidt thought he could save a little cash by living in his car," Abe recalls. "The

Cookie Gilchrist: One of the Bills' greatest players—and characters. *(Buffalo Bills)*

bottom line was he was cheap. He would take showers at the stadium, and park his car in the tunnel when the weather started becoming windy and cold.

"That was a tough neighborhood around War Memorial, but Schmidt never seemed worried about someone attacking him. He told me, 'Abe, nobody's going to bother somebody crazy enough to live in his car.'"

George Saimes. One of the greatest players in Bills history. Also one of the strangest. The four-time All-AFL safety was always analyzing things to death, according to Abe. "He had eighteen different pairs of football shoes, so he could make sure he had the right traction, depending on what field we were playing on. He'd change them several times a game, so we always had to make sure they were lined up and ready to go near the bench.

"He also did a lot of experimenting off the field. He ate sunflower seeds long before it became fashionable. And he used to mix motor oil with his shampoo because he had read where it would help stop hair loss."

Daryle Lamonica. Backed up Jack Kemp until 1968 when he was dealt to the Oakland Raiders in what still rates as the worst trade in club history. Lamonica, nicknamed the Mad Bomber, was a headstrong quarterback who loved doing things his way. "I remember one game [Coach Lou] Saban sent in a pass play, and Lamonica ran the ball instead and scored a touchdown," Abe recalls. "Lou went nuts on the sidelines, and Lamonica tried to calm him down by pointing out that he had scored a touchdown." It didn't work. Said Saban: "There are times when I think Daryle runs onto the field without his helmet on."

17 What Bills assistant coach played linebacker for the Kansas City Chiefs in the January 1, 1967 AFL title game at War Memorial Stadium?

●

18 Which Bills quarterback set an NFL record by throwing only one interception during an entire season?

●

19 What two defenders are known as the Bruise Brothers?

●

20 What teammate was center Kent Hull describing when he said: "He may be a teddy bear off the field, but on it, he's a grizzly."?

●

21 Who kicked the winning field goal in overtime during a 1980 game to beat the Los Angeles Rams, 10–7, and touch off a wild, post-game celebration at Rich Stadium?
a) John Leypoldt
b) Nick Mike-Mayer
c) Tom Dempsey
d) Booth Lusteg

●

22 What New York Mets catcher was chosen by the Bills in the 17th round of the 1973 draft?
a) Jerry Grote
b) Gary Carter
c) John Stearns
d) Yogi Berra

●

23 True or false: Jim Kelly was the first player chosen by the Bills in the 1983 draft.

●

24 Who holds the Bills record for most consecutive games throwing a touchdown pass?
a) Joe Ferguson
b) Jim Kelly
c) Jack Kemp
d) Dennis Shaw

●

25 Who was the first Arena Football League player to sign with the Bills?

•

26 What was the original name of the Buffalo team in the old All-American Football Conference?

•

27 What does the "C" stand for in Ralph C. Wilson's name?

•

28 This Bill said he was so determined that he was going to become a professional football player that he started practicing his autograph at the age of five.

•

29 Who blocked Jets kicker Pay Leahy's field goal attempt during the fourth quarter of the Bills' 9–6 overtime victory on November 20, 1988?

•

30 What NFL team did Jack Kemp originally play for?
   a)   Los Angeles Chargers
   b)   Buffalo Bills
   c)   Chicago Bears
   d)   Pittsburgh Steelers

•

31 What Bills defensive back restores classic cars as a hobby?

•

32 True or false: O. J. Simpson is the only Bill in the Hall of Fame.

•

33 What Bills player tied a pro football record when he recorded two safeties during the 1964 season?
   a)   Ron McDole
   b)   Paul Maguire
   c)   George Saimes
   d)   John Tracey

•

34 This quarterback once threw six touchdown passes against the Bills.
- a) Gary Hogeboom
- b) Dan Marino
- c) Daryle Lamonica
- d) John Hadl

●

35 From which team did the Bills claim Steve Tasker on waivers during the 1986 season?
- a) Kansas City Chiefs
- b) Chicago Bears
- c) Detroit Lions
- d) Houston Oilers

●

36 Who did the Bills play in their first regular season game on September 11, 1960 and what was the outcome?

●

37 Who did Dan Fouts hook up with for a 50-yard touchdown pass to give San Diego a 20–14 playoff victory against the Bills on January 3, 1981?
- a) Kellen Winslow
- b) Ron Smith
- c) Wes Chandler
- d) Chuck Muncie

●

38 True or false: The Bills made only one playoff appearance during the 1970s.

●

39 Match the player with his jersey number:

Mark Kelso	42
Butch Byrd	37
Steve Freeman	22
Nate Odomes	38

●

40 Who did Chuck Knox replace as Bills coach in 1978?
- a) Lou Saban
- b) Jim Ringo
- c) Buster Ramsey
- d) Joe Collier

●

LET'S MAKE
A DEAL

Here's a look at some of the best and worst trades in Bills history.

THE BEST

1978—O. J. Simpson to San Francisco for five draft choices. One of those picks was used to select Joe Cribbs, who wound up becoming the Bills' second all-time leading rusher. Another choice was used to select Tom Cousineau. He, of course, never signed with Buffalo, but that turned out to be a blessing because when the Bills traded Cousineau's rights to Cleveland, they acquired a first-round draft pick which they used to select Jim Kelly in 1983. The Bills also used one of the five picks on Ken Johnson, who was a solid contributor at defensive end for several seasons. Juice was at the end of his career when Buffalo unloaded him, so the Bills made out like bandits.

1977—Tight end Paul Seymour to the Pittsburgh Steelers for wide receiver Frank Lewis. Lewis set a club record with two 1,000-yard receiving seasons. Seymour never played for the Steelers.

1987—Greg Bell and three high draft choices to Indianapolis for linebacker Cornelius Bennett. Only time will tell, but this bold deal by Bills General Manager Bill Polian could go down as the best trade in Bills history. Sure, the Bills parted with an awful lot, but few players have had as much of an impact as Bennett has had in such a short period of time. He blossomed into an All-Pro player in only his second season, and improved those around him. His presence took some of the multiple-team blocking load off of defensive end Bruce Smith and enabled Shane Conlan to move to inside linebacker, where he has won All-Pro and Rookie-of-the-Year honors.

1960—Defensive tackle Al Crow to the Boston Patriots for running back Wray Carlton. Crow vanished from the scene. Carlton became the Bills' third all-time leading ground-gainer.

Bills linebacker Cornelius Bennett gets ready to run down another ballcarrier.
(Robert L. Smith)

1974—Quarterback Dennis Shaw to St. Louis for wide receiver Ahmad Rashad. Shaw was on his way out. Rashad was one of the NFL's most dangerous receivers during his two seasons with the Bills.

1988—Roland Mitchell and a sixth-round draft choice to Phoenix for strong safety Leonard Smith. More highway robbery by Polian. Mitchell, a seldom-used cornerback, didn't fit into the Bills' picture. Smith, a Pro Bowl-caliber player, provided secondary with much needed hit man.

1988—Two middle-round draft choices to the Kansas City Chiefs for defensive end Art Still. Some suggested Still was washed up, but the four-time Pro Bowler silenced skeptics with an outstanding season.

THE WORST

1967—Daryle Lamonica and Glenn Bass to the Oakland Raiders for Tom Flores and Art Powell. Ralph Wilson still has nightmares about this one. Lamonica took the Raiders to the Super Bowl in 1968. Flores was injury-prone and played only two seasons with the Bills. Powell, who once caught 16 touchdown passes in a season with Raiders, was over-the-hill and lasted only one year in Buffalo.

1971—Ron McDole to the Washington Redskins for draft choices used to select Bob Kampa, Jeff Yeates, and John Ford. Bills mistakenly thought McDole was through, but the big defensive lineman had eight quality seasons with the Redskins Over-the-Hill Gang and was named to their all-time team. Kampa, Yeates, and Ford vanished from the scene.

1980—Offensive guard Joe DeLamielleure to Cleveland for the Browns' second-round pick in 1981 and third-round selection in 1982. Buffalo used the '81 pick on L.S.U. defensive back Chris Williams and traded the '82 pick to Seattle for guard Tom Lynch. Neither player did much with the Bills. DeLamielleure wound up having several more productive seasons with the Browns before ending his career back in Buffalo.

1980—Wide receiver Bobby Chandler to the Raiders for linebacker Phil Villapiano. Villapiano was in the twilight of his career. Chandler caught 10 touchdown passes to help the Raiders to another Super Bowl.

41 What famous athlete co-starred with O. J. Simpson in the Hertz Rent-a-Car commercials?

●

42 What Bills receiver began his career as a quarterback with the Denver Broncos?

●

43 Who did the Bills play in the final game at War Memorial Stadium on December 10, 1972?

a) Detroit Lions   c) Cincinnati Bengals
b) New York Jets   d) Miami Dolphins

●

44 During the first exhibition game played at Rich Stadium in 1973, this Washington Redskin returned the opening kickoff for a touchdown. Who was he?

●

45 True or false: O. J. Simpson was the first Heisman Trophy winner to lead the NFL in rushing.

●

46 What were Ralph Wilson and the founding fathers of the American Football League known as?

●

47 Name the two former Bills head coaches who once played for the Green Bay Packers.

a) Jim Ringo and Elijah Pitts
b) Jim Ringo and Hank Bullough
c) Jim Ringo and Buster Ramsey
d) Jim Ringo and Lou Saban

●

48 In a September 29, 1974 game at Shea Stadium the Bills offense went an entire game without one of these:

a) a first down   c) a penalty
b) a pass completion   d) a fumble

●

49 This Bills general manager was an award-winning sports columnist for the Milwaukee *Journal.*

●

50 On November 30, 1986, the Bills defeated this team, 17–14, to snap the second longest road losing streak in league history at 22 games.

1. b) Jack Kemp.
2. b) Art Still.
3. False. The NFL record is 12, shared by Bert Jones of the Baltimore Colts and Warren Moon of the Houston Oilers.
4. c) Bo Roberson. The former Cornell star played one season with the Bills, leading the team in receptions with 31 for 483 yards and three touchdowns.
5. a) *The Towering Inferno.*
6. True. The Jets appeared in Super Bowl III; the Colts in III and V; the Patriots in XX; the Dolphins in V, VI, VII, VIII, XVII.
7. Guards Reggie McKenzie and Joe DeLamielleure, centers Bruce Jarvis and Mike Montler, tackles Donnie Green and Dave Foley, and tight end Paul Seymour. Jarvis played the first eight games before being sidelined by a knee injury.
8. Henry Schmidt.
9. George Steinbrenner.
10. d) John Kidd.
11. Quarterback Jim Kelly (Houston Gamblers); center Kent Hull (New Jersey Generals); Trumaine Johnson (Arizona Wranglers); kicker Scott Norwood (Birmingham Stallions); and linebacker Ray Bentley (Michigan Panthers).
12. True. Norwood was 0–6 from 50-yards and beyond entering the 1989 season.
13. b) Roland Hooks.
14. Shane Conlan was named for the main character in the movie *Shane.*
15. Joe Danelo.
16. George Saimes and Elbert Dubenion.
17. Bills defensive coordinator Walt Corey.
18. Joe Ferguson threw only one interception in 151 attempts during the 1976 season.
19. Bruce Smith and Cornelius Bennett.
20. Fred Smerlas.
21. b) Nick Mike-Mayer.
22. c) John Stearns.
23. False. The Bills used the 12th pick overall on tight end Tony Hunter. Kelly was the 14th pick overall.
24. b) Jim Kelly. His 18-game streak ran from November 2, 1986 through December 14, 1987.

Elbert Dubenion remains the Bills all-time receiving leader, 21 years after his retirement in 1968. *(Buffalo Bills)*

25. Defensive back Durwood Roquemore, who played for the Chicago Bruisers.

26. The Bisons.

27. Cookerly.

28. Jim Kelly.

29. Fred Smerlas.

30. d) Pittsburgh Steelers.

31. Leonard Smith.

32. True.

33. a) Ron McDole.

34. c) Daryle Lamonica.

35. d) Houston Oilers.

36. The Bills lost to the New York Titans, 27–3, before an announced crowd of 10,200 fans at the Polo Grounds on September 11, 1960.

37. b) Ron Smith.

38. True. The Bills only playoff appearance of the 1970s came after the 1974 season.

39. Mark Kelso, 38; Butch Byrd, 42; Steve Freeman, 22; Nate Odomes, 37.

40. b) Jim Ringo.

41. Arnold Palmer.

42. Marlin Briscoe.

43. a) Detroit Lions. The game ended in a 21–21 tie as O. J. Simpson rushed for 116 yards.

44. Herb Mul-Key.

45. False. Alan Ameche, who won the Heisman at the University of Wisconsin in 1954, led the NFL in rushing during his rookie season.

46. The Foolish Club.

47. b) Jim Ringo and Hank Bullough.

48. b) a pass completion.

49. Terry Bledsoe.

50. Kansas City Chiefs.

HALFTIME

30 Years of Pro Football
1960   1989

TM / © 1989

O. J. SIMPSON:
MR. BUFFALO BILL

O. J. Simpson accomplished so much during his career with the Bills that it's easy to forget the early years when breakaway runs and victories occurred about as often as Halley's Comet. After three mediocre seasons, O. J.—"Stutter-Step," as he was derisively known to his critics—wanted out of Buffalo. "I figured my dreams of becoming a Hall of Famer were dead," he explained.

They were until Coach Lou Saban arrived in Buffalo in 1972.

"You don't make a decoy or a wide receiver out of one of the most talented running backs to play the game," said Saban, alluding to the misguided approach employed by his predecessor, John Rauch. "The strategy with a back the caliber of O. J. isn't complicated. You simply give him the football and let him run."

O. J. took the football from Saban and didn't stop running until he reached the Pro Football Hall of Fame.

These days, the Juice makes his living in Hollywood, acting, producing, and promoting products.

Here's a look at some of his football records and movie and television acting credits.

What's wrong with this picture? Why, O. J. Simpson's jersey number, of course. The Juice was forced to wear No. 36 during his rookie training camp because Gary McDermott was already wearing No. 32. McDermott was cut that year, enabling Simpson to reclaim the jersey number he wore during his college career at Southern California. *(Professional Football Hall of Fame)*

The Juice on the loose. *(Buffalo Bills)*

BILLS RECORDS HELD BY THE JUICE

CAREER

Most points scored: 420
Most touchdowns: 70
Most rushing touchdowns: 57
Most rushing attempts: 2,123
Most rushing yards gained: 10,183
Best rushing average: 4.8 per carry
Most combined yards: 11,107
Most 200-yard rushing games: 7
Most 1,000-yard rushing seasons: 5 (1972–76)
Most seasons leading the team in rushing: 9 (1969–77)
Most Pro Bowl appearances: 5 (shares record with Joe DeLamielleure and Fred Smerlas)

Here's O. J. in action during an exhibition game against the Detroit Lions in his rookie year. Notice that Juice was wearing No. 36 instead of his normal No. 32. *(Professional Football Hall of Fame)*

SEASON

Most points: 138 in 1975
Most touchdowns: 23 in 1975
Most rushing touchdowns: 16 in 1975
Most consecutive games with a touchdown: 14 (from September 21, 1975 to December 20, 1975)
Most consecutive games with a rushing touchdown: 7 (November 9, 1975 to December 20, 1975)
Most rushing attempts: 332 in 1973
Most rushing yards: 2,003 in 1973
Best rushing average: 6.0 in 1973
Most 200-yard rushing games: 3

GAME

Most rushing attempts: 39 vs. Kansas City, October 29, 1973
Most rushing yards: 273 vs. Detroit, Thanksgiving Day, 1976
Longest run: 94 yards vs. Pittsburgh, October 29, 1972
Best kickoff return average: 70.5 (two returns for 141 yards vs. Jets, October 4, 1970)

1973—2,003 YARDS: A FOOTBALL ODYSSEY

Date	Opponent	Carries	Yards	Avg.	TDs
S. 16	New England	29	250	8.6	2
S. 23	San Diego	22	103	4.7	1
S. 30	New York Jets	24	123	5.1	0
O. 7	Philadelphia	27	171	6.3	1
O. 14	Baltimore	22	166	7.5	2
O. 21	Miami	14	55	3.9	0
O. 29	Kansas City	39	157	4.0	2
N. 4	New Orleans	20	79	3.9	0
N. 11	Cincinnati	20	99	4.9	1
N. 18	Miami	20	120	6.0	0
N. 25	Baltimore	15	124	8.3	1
D. 2	Atlanta	24	137	5.7	0
D. 9	New England	22	219	10.0	1
D. 16	New York Jets	34	200	6.0	1
TOTALS:		332	2,003	6.0	12

O. J. ON THE SILVER SCREEN AND THE LITTLE SCREEN

Movies
Feature films—*The Towering Inferno* (1974); *The Klansman* (1974); *Killer Force* (1975); *Capricorn* (1977); *Firepower* (1978); *Hambone and Hilly* (1983); *The Naked Gun* (1988).
Others—*Goldie and the Boxer* (1979); *Detour to Terror* (1980); *Goldie and the Boxer Go to Hollywood* (1981); *Cocaine and Blue Eyes* (1982).

JERNIGAN

O. J. Simpson made his movie acting debut in *The Towering Inferno* in 1974. The Juice played Jerrigan, the chief security officer of the world's tallest skyscraper. *(20th Century-Fox Film Corporation)*

Television
Variety—"Lucy Show," "Flip Wilson," "Sonny and Cher"; Bob Hope, Mac Davis.
Drama—"Medical Center," "Owen Marshall," "Cade's County," "A Killing Affair," "Roots."
Specials—Academy Awards, Emmy Awards, "Saturday Night Live."
Sports—1976 and '84 Summer Olympics; "Wide World of Sports"; "ABC Monday Night Football"; Superstars; NBC's NFL Live.

THIRD
QUARTER

BUFFALO BILLS

1960   30 Years of Pro Football   1989

TM / © 1989

1   What coach said of Jim Kelly: "He needs the chickens around him to get it done. He just can't go in and make chicken salad out of goosemunk."?

●

2   True or false: Joe Ferguson and Jack Kemp threw more interceptions than touchdown passes during their careers with the Bills.

●

3   Where did Cookie Gilchrist play college football?

●

4   On August 8, 1961, the Bills played the Hamilton Tiger-Cats of the Canadian Football League in an exhibition game. What was the outcome?

●

5   During the 1988 season, the Bills added a third Penn State linebacker to their roster, prompting Marv Levy to joke: "As Gloria Vanderbilt used to say, you can never be too rich, too thin, or have too many Penn State linebackers." Name the three Penn State linebackers who played for the Bills in '88.

●

6   Who recruited Paul Maguire to play football at The Citadel?
   a)   George Steinbrenner   c)   Al Davis
   b)   Vince Lombardi   d)   Ralph Wilson

●

7   From October 18, 1964, until November 7, 1965, the Bills defense didn't allow one of these:
   a)   a first down   c)   a rushing touchdown
   b)   a touchdown pass   d)   a field goal

●

8   In 1988, Kent Hull was voted into the Pro Bowl, becoming the first Bills offensive lineman to be so honored since (fill in the blank) in 1979.
   a)   Reggie McKenzie   c)   Will Grant
   b)   Joe DeLamielleure   d)   Donnie Green

●

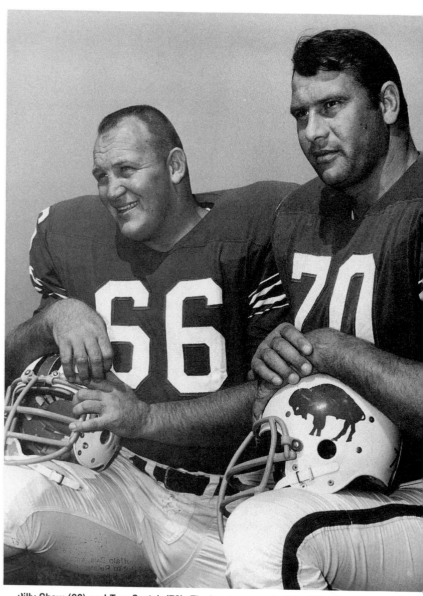

Billy Shaw (66) and Tom Sestak (70): The heart and soul of the Bills AFL title teams. *(Buffalo Bills)*

9 Who scored the Bills' first touchdown in a July 30, 1960, exhibition game against the Boston Patriots at War Memorial Stadium?

●

10 What Bills wide receiver caught a touchdown pass in the waning moments of a 1974 game to hand the Raiders their first Monday Night Football loss?
a) Ahmad Rashad
b) J. D. Hill
c) Lou Piccone
d) Bobby Chandler

●

11 What controversial penalty nullified a first down completion from Joe Ferguson to Lou Piccone in the final minutes of a 28–21 loss to the Cincinnati Bengals in their AFC semifinal playoff game on January 3, 1982?
a) backfield in motion
b) delay of game
c) unnecessary roughness
d) too many men on the field

●

12 What three-time Pro Bowl cornerback did Elbert Dubenion discover while working as a scout for the Bills?

●

13 Who became so angry during the Jim Kelly contract talks that he reportedly got down in a three-point stance and challenged one of the negotiators to try to get by him?

●

14 True or false: O. J. Simpson and Jack Kemp are the only Buffalo players to have their numbers retired.

●

15 Name the Hall of Fame receiver who caught four passes for 116 yards in the New York Titans' 27–3 victory against the Bills in the first game played by the teams in 1960.

●

16 What Bill defensive lineman went on to become a professional slow-pitch softball star?

●

FRED SMERLAS:
LOCKER-ROOM POET

It doesn't matter whether Fred Smerlas makes 10 tackles or none: You'll usually find a flock of reporters around his locker after a Buffalo Bills game. The ten-year veteran always has been a media darling because he is a witty athlete able to go beyond the clichés and offer unique perspective.

Here's a sampler of some classic Freddyisms:

On teammate Bruce Smith: "He hits like a bear and dances like a ballerina."

On the lean years with the Bills: "When we were 2–14, the only things that showed up at Rich Stadium on Sundays were the snowflakes."

On forcing William "The Fridge" Perry's first fumble during an exhibition game in 1986: "When I saw the fat guy coming my way, I buried my head in his belly button. I didn't see daylight for five minutes."

On the replacement players who filled NFL rosters during the 1987 players' strike: "They're dead men. Just look at it this way: If the truckers went on strike and they had scabs come in, how many new lily pads would there be in Lake Erie?"

On Fred Smerlas, the football player: "When I go on the field, my hair's messed up, I need a shave, my shirt's out, I have old shoes on, I have blood all over my hands. I look ugly and I play ugly."

On teammate Howard Ballard's block of a field goal attempt: "We put a little barbecue sauce on the ball, told him it was a chicken wing and he just grabbed it out of the air."

On the toughness of Jim Kelly: "He's just an old hammerhead. He'll drink with the best of the boys and he'll slug it out with them. He don't care. When he throws an interception, who's the first guy out there trying to make the tackle? It's Kelly trying to take their heads off. Most quarterbacks would fall flat on the ground or run off the field. He's not like that."

Nose tackle Fred Smerlas sizes up the opposition. *(Robert L. Smith)*

17 What former member of Syracuse University's 1959 national championship team is a member of the Bills Silver Anniversary team?

●

18 The Bills have had the first draft pick overall five times. Name the picks and the years.

●

19 Match the coach with his alma mater:

Marv Levy   Juniata (Pennsylvania) College

Chuck Knox   William and Mary
Kay Stephenson   Coe (Iowa) College
Harvey Johnson   University of Florida

●

20 What Bills coach once converted 146 consecutive extra points while playing with the New York Yankees in the old All-American Football Conference?
a) Lou Saban
b) Harvey Johnson
c) Joe Collier
d) John Rauch

●

21 Scott Norwood scored 129 points in 1988 to become only the fourth Buffalo player to surpass the century mark in scoring. Name the other three.

●

22 What two receivers share the club record for most touchdown receptions in a season?
a) Jerry Butler and Frank Lewis
b) Frank Lewis and Elbert Dubenion
c) Elbert Dubenion and Bobby Chandler
d) Bobby Chandler and Glenn Bass

●

23 In what season did the Bills first wear their red helmets?
a) 1984   c) 1973
b) 1980   d) 1962

●

24 True or false: Jack Kemp is the AFL's all-time passing yardage leader.

●

25 Which Bills quarterback is colorblind?
a) Joe Ferguson
b) Jack Kemp
c) Jim Kelly
d) Daryle Lamonica

●

26 What Canadian Football League team did Tom Cousineau play for?
a) Montreal Alouettes
b) Toronto Argonauts
c) Edmonton Oilers
d) Calgary Roughriders

●

27 True or false: The 1988 Bills set a team record with 46 sacks.

●

28 Who holds the club record for most receptions in a season by a tight end?
a) Ernie Warlick
b) Pete Metzelaars
c) Eason Ramson
d) Reuben Gant

●

29 Who did the Bills acquire in the 1980 deal that sent Bobby Chandler to the Oakland Raiders?

●

30 Which of the following running backs had the fewest rushing yards during his rookie season with the Bills?
a) Cookie Gilchrist
b) O. J. Simpson
c) Greg Bell
d) Thurman Thomas

●

31 True or false: Scott Norwood is the only Bills kicker to compete in a Pro Bowl.

●

32 What wide receiver suffered a career-ending leg injury while catching a 25-yard touchdown pass in a 1986 game against the Miami Dolphins?

●

33 What unusual hobby does Bills trainer Ed Abramoski engage in away from football?

●

34 Ten men have coached the Bills. Only three of them have career winning records with the team. Who are they?

●

35 True or false: The Bills did not play in the first regular season NFL game at War Memorial Stadium.

●

36 Match the player with his college coach:

Reggie McKenzie	Duffy Daugherty
Joe Ferguson	Ray Perkins
Cornelius Bennett	Ara Parseghian
Joe DeLamielleure	Frank Broyles
Walt Patulski	Bo Schembechler

●

37 What position did Marv Levy play in college?

●

38 What quarterback had his 30-game touchdown streak snapped against the Bills in a 1987 game?

●

39 What was the Bills record during the three strike games in 1987?

●

40 What year was O. J. Simpson inducted into the Pro Football Hall of Fame?

●

41 Who was Bills offensive guard Billy Shaw talking about when he said: "When you play against (blank) in practice every day, you either improve or retire."?

●

LOU SABAN:
THE MARCO POLO
OF COACHING

Lou Saban coached the Bills to two American Football League titles and is credited with salvaging O. J. Simpson's career. But he's best known for something else—his disappearing act. Since 1950, Saban has worked nineteen jobs. His journeys have taken him to three pro-football teams, seven colleges and three high schools. Sport's most famous nomad also has managed a race track and served as president of a major league baseball team. In a 1986 *Los Angeles Times* story, Saban was described as "the Marco Polo of coaching, the Sultan of Sayonara. Now you see him, now you don't." His updated job resume follows.

1950–52 Coach, Case Institute of Technology, 10–13–1 record.
1953 Assistant coach, University of Washington.
1954–55 Assistant and head coach, Northwestern University. Guided Wildcats to 0–8–1 record in 1955.
1957–59 Coach, Western Illinois University, 20–5–1 record.
1960–61 Coach, Boston Patriots, 7–12 record.
1962–65 Coach, Buffalo Bills, 38–18–3 record. American Football League titles in 1964–65.
1966 Coach, University of Maryland, 4–6 record.
1967–71 Coach, Denver Broncos, 20–42–3 record.
1972–76 Coach, Buffalo Bills, 32–29–1 record.
1976 Athletic director, University of Cincinnati.
1977–78 Coach, University of Miami (Fla.), 9–13 record.
1979 Coach, Army. 2–8–1 record.
1980–81 Manager, Tampa Bay (Florida) Downs racetrack. Resigned when New York Yankees owner George Steinbrenner gave him a promotion.
1981–82 President, New York Yankees.
1982–86 Scout, New York Yankees.
1983–84 Coach, University of Central Florida, 6–10 record.
1986–87 Assistant coach, business education teacher, Martin County (Florida) High School.
1988 Head coach, South Fork High School, Stuart, Florida.
1989 Head coach, Georgetown (South Carolina) High School.

42 In 1989, Ralph Wilson became the second non-player to have his name placed on the Rich Stadium Wall of Fame. Who is the other non-player up there?

•

43 Who is the Bills' all-time receiving leader?
a) Jerry Butler
b) Bobby Chandler
c) Elbert Dubenion
d) Glenn Bass

•

44 This former fourth-round draft pick of the NBA's Boston Celtics had an unsuccessful tryout as a tight end with the Bills during their 1987 training camp.

•

45 Against which team did Joe Ferguson injure his ankle in the second-to-last regular season game in 1980, hindering the Bills' attempt at making the Super Bowl?
a) New England
b) Miami
c) San Francisco
d) Baltimore

•

46 Who replaced Joe Ferguson at quarterback following his 1980 ankle injury?

•

47 How many playoff games did O. J. Simpson play in?

•

48 Name the Bills quarterback born on Valentine's Day.

•

49 Name the five quarterbacks who saw action for the Bills after Jack Kemp suffered a season-ending injury during the 1968 training camp.

•

50 What backup quarterback served as the Bills punter in 1963?

Joe Cribbs was the focal point of the Bills offense during the early 1980s.
(Buffalo Bills)

THIRD QUARTER—ANSWERS

1. Hank Bullough.

2. True. Ferguson threw 190 interceptions and 181 touchdowns, while Kemp had 77 touchdowns and 132 interceptions.

3. Nowhere. Gilchrist was one of several Bills players who never played college football.

4. The Tiger-Cats won, 38–21.

5. Shane Conlan, Scott Radecic, and Don Graham.

6. c) Al Davis.

7. c) a rushing touchdown.

8. b) Joe DeLamielleure.

9. Fullback Maurice Bassett in a 28–7 loss. He was cut two days later.

10. a) Ahmad Rashad.

11. b) delay of game.

12. Robert James.

13. Bill Polian.

14. False. Although O. J.'s 32 and Kemp's 15 haven't been issued in recent years, no Bills uniform had officially been retired through the 1988 season.

15. Don Maynard.

16. Scott Virkus.

17. Al Bemiller.

18. Ken Rice, offensive lineman, 1961; O. J. Simpson, running back, 1969; Walt Patulski, defensive tackle, 1972; Tom Cousineau, linebacker, 1979; Bruce Smith, defensive end, 1985.

19. Marv Levy, Coe (Iowa) College; Chuck Knox, Juniata (Pennsylvania) College; Kay Stephenson, University of Florida; Harvey Johnson, William and Mary.

20. b) Harvey Johnson.

21. Cookie Gilchrist scored 128 in 1962; Pete Gogolak had 102 in 1964 and 115 in '65; O. J. Simpson had 138 in 1975.

22. c) Elbert Dubenion scored 10 in 1964 while Bobby Chandler scored 10 in 1976.

23. a) 1984.

24. True. During his 10-year AFL career with first the Chargers, then the Bills, Kemp passed for 21,130 yards.

25. c) Jim Kelly.

26. a) Montreal Alouettes.

27. False. The 1981 club had 47.

28. b) Pete Metzelaars had 49 receptions in 1986.
29. Linebacker Phil Villapiano.
30. b) O. J. Simpson.
31. True.
32. Jerry Butler.
33. He races homing pigeons.
34. Lou Saban (68–45–4); Chuck Knox (37–36) and Marv Levy (21–17).
35. True. The first regular-season NFL game in War Memorial Stadium came on September 14, 1938, between the Pittsburgh Pirates and Philadelphia Eagles. In fact, War Memorial hosted at least six regular-season NFL games before the Bills made their debut.
36. Reggie McKenzie—Bo Schembechler; Joe Ferguson—Frank Broyles; Cornelius Bennett—Ray Perkins; Joe De-Lamielleure—Duffy Daugherty; Walt Patulski—Ara Parseghian.
37. Running back.
38. Dan Marino.
39. One win, two losses.
40. 1985.
41. Tom Sestak.
42. Patrick McGroder.
43. c) Elbert Dubenion with 296 receptions.
44. Clif Webber.
45. a) New England.
46. Dan Manucci.
47. One, a 32–14 loss to the Super Bowl champion Pittsburgh Steelers on December 22, 1974.
48. Jim Kelly.
49. Dan Darragh, Ed Rutkowski, Kay Stephenson, Tom Flores, and Benny Russell.
50. Daryle Lamonica.

FOURTH
QUARTER

TM / © 1989

1 What was Preston Ridlehuber's claim to fame?

●

2 Name the former World War II intelligence officer and Bills coach who once gave his players a pep talk in Chinese.

●

3 What Bills offensive lineman did former New York Jets star Mark Gastineau dread going against?
   a) Conrad Dobler
   b) Will Grant
   c) Joe Devlin
   d) Reggie McKenzie

●

4 Who was Lou Saban referring to when he said: "Sometimes he goes onto the field without his helmet on."?
   a) Cookie Gilchrist
   b) Daryle Lamonica
   c) George Saimes
   d) Ron McDole

●

5 True or false: Paul Maguire holds the club record for highest punting average in a season.

●

6 This Bill made 17 tackles, including 4 sacks, and forced 3 fumbles in a 1987 game against the Philadelphia Eagles, prompting defensive coordinator Walt Corey to marvel: "They ought to put a film of that game in a time capsule." Name the player.

●

7 What's the only team that has never played an exhibition or regular-season game at Rich Stadium?
   a) Detroit Lions
   b) San Francisco 49ers
   c) Seattle Seahawks
   d) New York Giants

●

A quarterback's worst nightmare: Bruce Smith raging in unblocked. *(Robert L. Smith)*

8 This former Bill became the first black ever to start an NFL season-opener at quarterback.
- a) Marlin Briscoe
- b) James Harris
- c) Willie Thrower
- d) Doug Williams

●

9 What's the name of the cartoon character created by Bills linebacker-author Ray Bentley?

●

10 What Bill once appeared on "Late Night with David Letterman"?

●

11 How many times did Joe Ferguson guide the Bills into the playoffs?
- a) one
- b) two
- c) three
- d) four

●

12 Name the player who led the Bills in receiving in 1988 despite playing most of the year with a protective cast on his broken wrist.

●

13 Two of Ronnie Harmon's brothers have played in the NFL. Who are they?

●

14 True or false: Linebacker Shane Nelson wasn't drafted out of college.

●

15 Who is the only Buffalo player to become a Bills head coach?

●

16 What was the only team the Bills defeated during their dreadful 1971 season?

●

MOVE OVER,
YOGI

During his one and a half seasons as head coach of the Bills, Hank Bullough fought a losing battle against National Football League opponents and the Mother Tongue.

His teams won only 4 of 21 games before he was fired on November 3, 1986. His record with the English language wasn't much better.

Like Yogi Berra, Bullough unintentionally entertained fans and reporters with humorous malaprops. He often praised his team's "work ethnic" and talked about making decisions on the "spare of the moment."

After a loss to the Jets, he said a long-pass play had taken "the sails right out of our wind." That still ranks as one of his all-time best.

Here's a look at some other memorable Bulloughprops:

On his team's progress: "We keep beating ourselves, but we're getting better at it."

On a question about whether Jim Kelly's multi-million dollar contract was insured: "You mean with Lords of London?"

On the Bills plans in a college draft that featured Bo Jackson and Napoleon McCallum: "Well, you've got that Jackson kid at Auburn and that Napoleon Bonaparte kid at Navy."

On interference from Bills owner Ralph Wilson: "I'm not a yes guy. He knew that when I hired him."

On playing well, but losing: "I don't believe in morale victories."

On a question from a belligerent caller about the length of his contract: "I don't wish to indulge that information."

On the lack of response to his hiring of a new assistant coach: "I haven't exactly been divulged with phone calls."

On the development of one of his quarterbacks: "He's making improvement throwing the ball where he's throwing the ball."

17   Who was former team physician Dr. Joseph Godfrey talking about when he said: "He has seventy-year-old knees on a thirty-year-old body."?

●

18   Match the player with his alma mater:

Leonard Smith   Memphis State
George Saimes   Mississippi State
Steve Freeman   Michigan State
Butch Byrd   McNeese State
Derrick Burroughs   Boston University

●

19   True or false: Jim Kelly's first football game at Rich Stadium came during his NFL debut against the Jets on September 7, 1986.

●

20   Name the three Canadian Football League teams that employed Cookie Gilchrist.

●

21   Who was the first player signed by the Bills?
   a)   Richie Lucas
   b)   Joe Schaffer
   c)   Billy Shaw
   d)   Art Baker

●

22   What defensive back set a club record when he returned an interception 101 yards in a 1976 game against Kansas City?
   a)   Tony Greene
   b)   Steve Freeman
   c)   Robert James
   d)   Charles Romes

●

23   Who was Marv Levy talking about when he said: "He's one of those old-time, blood-and-mud-type football players. He reminds me tremendously of Jack Lambert. He is very much the same type of player, right down to those skinny legs."?

●

24 Name the Bill who helped form the American Football League Players' Association and served as its president for five years.

•

25 How many times have the Rich Stadium goal posts been torn down by jubilant fans?

•

26 Who was the first punter drafted by the Bills?
a) Paul Maguire
b) Brian Doherty
c) Marv Bateman
d) Greg Carter

•

27 What's Butch Byrd's real first name?

•

28 Who is the third-leading rusher in Bills history?
a) Wray Carlton
b) Cookie Gilchrist
c) Greg Bell
d) Jim Braxton

•

29 Name the Bill who captained an 0–11 football team during his senior year of college.

•

30 What 6'6", 313-pound offensive lineman is nicknamed "House" and "Howard Huge"?

•

31 What former Syracuse University star returned three punts for touchdowns during his career with the Bills and established a club record with a 91-yard return in a 1977 game against Cleveland?

•

32 Name the two NFL teams that Jim Kelly's older brother, Pat, played linebacker for.

•

33 Which sack dance did Bruce Smith perform first at Rich Stadium—the Fred Sanford Sack Attack or the Pee Wee Herman?

•

34 What coach has the poorest career won-lost record with the Bills?
   a) Harvey Johnson
   b) Kay Stephenson
   c) Jim Ringo
   d) Hank Bullough

●

35 True or false: Marv Levy originally interviewed for the Bills head coaching job after Chuck Knox departed for Seattle following the 1982 season.

●

36 How many touchdown passes did Jim Kelly throw during his two seasons in the United States Football League?
   a) 83
   b) 73
   c) 49
   d) 57

●

37 Which running back set the club record for most rushing yards by a rookie in a season?
   a) Greg Bell
   b) Terry Miller
   c) Cookie Gilchrist
   d) Joe Cribbs

●

38 True or false: Joe DeLamielleure is not a member of the Bills Silver Anniversary team.

●

39 What team did Elbert Dubenion originally sign with?

●

40 Who holds the Bills record with 13 consecutive field goals?
   a) Nick Mike-Mayer
   b) Pete Gogolak
   c) Scott Norwood
   d) John Leypoldt

●

41 How many touchdowns did Jerry Butler score during his record-setting game against the Jets in 1979?

●

42 What two quarterbacks did Coach Buster Ramsey alternate during the Bills' first season?

●

43 What Buffalo News editor played a prominent role in bringing an AFL team to Buffalo?
   a) Larry Felser
   b) Paul Neville
   c) Charley Young
   d) Vic Carucci

●

44 Who led the Bills in tackles in 1988?
   a) Shane Conlan
   b) Cornelius Bennett
   c) Scott Radecic
   d) Ray Bentley

●

45 What kicker took over for Pete Gogolak when he jumped to the NFL's New York Giants following the 1966 season?

●

46 What Bills running back wore leg braces as a child?

●

47 Name the four players who started on the Bills defensive line during their two championship seasons in the mid-1960s.

●

48 What song was blaring over the loudspeakers during the Bills chorus-line celebration following their stirring 10–7 overtime win against the Los Angeles Rams in 1980?
   a) "We Can Make It Happen"
   b) "Shout"
   c) "Talking Proud"
   d) "Celebration"

●

49 What Bills linebacker said: "Where else could you go out on Sunday and run around acting like a kid? If you did that out on the street they'd put you in a mental ward. On the field you can spit, cuss, wipe your nose—whatever—and nobody notices."?

    a) Shane Conlan
    b) Shane Nelson
    c) Darryl Talley
    d) Cornelius Bennett

●

50 What Bill intercepted two of Vinny Testaverde's passes during the 1987 Fiesta Bowl?

Pro Bowl linebacker Shane Conlan takes a well-deserved break during training camp. *(Robert L. Smith)*

FOURTH QUARTER—ANSWERS

1. The little-known running back came off the bench in the fourth quarter of a 1969 game and threw a 48-yard touchdown pass to Haven Moses as the Bills defeated the Patriots, 23–16, one of the few highlights in a 4–10 season.

2. Lou Saban.

3. c) Joe Devlin.

4. b) Daryle Lamonica.

5. False. Billy Atkins set the record when he averaged 45 yards per punt in 1961. Maguire's best was 44.5 in 1969.

6. Cornelius Bennett.

7. c) Seattle Seahawks.

8. b) James Harris.

9. Darby the Dinosaur.

10. Jim Kelly.

11. c) Three. 1974, 1980, and 1981.

12. Andre Reed.

13. Older brother Derrick Harmon played several years with the San Francisco 49ers, while younger brother Kevin is a member of the Seattle Seahawks.

14. True. Nelson had an offer to try out with the Dallas Cowboys, but chose the Bills instead and wound up leading the team in tackles and earning All-Rookie honors in 1977.

15. Kay Stephenson.

16. They beat New England, 27–20, behind J. D. Hill's two touchdown receptions.

17. Tom Sestak.

18. Leonard Smith, McNeese State; George Saimes, Michigan State; Steve Freeman, Mississippi State; Butch Byrd, Boston University; and Derrick Burroughs, Memphis State.

19. False. Kelly played once at Rich Stadium during his collegiate career. His University of Miami team lost to Syracuse, 25–15, at Rich Stadium during the 1979 season.

20. Hamilton, Saskatchewan, and Toronto.

21. b) Tennessee tackle Joe Schaffer signed with the Bills on December 5, 1959.

22. a) Tony Greene.

23. Shane Conlan.

24. Jack Kemp.

25. Twice. The first time occurred on September 7, 1980, after the Bills defeated the Miami Dolphins to snap a 20-game series losing streak. The other time occurred following the Bills' title-clinching victory against the New York Jets on November 20, 1988.

26. b) Brian Doherty.

27. George Butch Byrd.

28. Wray Carlton with 3,368 yards.

29. Fred Smerlas was captain of a Boston College team that went winless in 1979.

30. Howard Ballard.

31. Keith Moody.

32. Baltimore Colts and Detroit Lions.

33. The Pee Wee Herman.

34. a) Harvey Johnson by a whisker. Johnson compiled a 2–23–1 record in two seasons with the team. Jim Ringo was 3–20, Bullough 4–17, and Stephenson 10–26.

35. True. Levy had an amicable interview with Ralph Wilson, but the owner decided to promote Kay Stephenson.

36. a) 83.

37. d) Joe Cribbs with 1,185 in 1980.

38. True. The guards are Billy Shaw and Reggie McKenzie.

39. The Cleveland Browns.

40. c) Scott Norwood.

41. Four.

42. Tommy O'Connell and John Green.

43. b) Paul Neville.

44. d) Ray Bentley.

45. Booth Lusteg.

46. O. J. Simpson.

47. Tackles Tom Sestak and Jim Dunaway, and ends Ron McDole and Tom Day.

48. c) Talking Proud.

49. c) Darryl Talley.

50. Shane Conlan.

OVERTIME

1 What Bills defensive back led the AFL in interceptions (10) and punting average (45.0) during the 1961 season?
   a) George Saimes
   b) Butch Byrd
   c) Billy Atkins
   d) Richie Lucas

●

2 True or false: One of the draft picks acquired in the 1978 trade of O. J. Simpson to the San Francisco 49ers indirectly led to the selection of Jim Kelly in 1983.

●

3 Who said during the 1988 season: "They used to throw their game programs at me. Now they are asking me to sign them."?

●

4 Name the running back who was unable to take part in any contact drills during his first practice with the Bills because the team didn't have a helmet large enough to fit him.

●

5 From how many points behind did the Bills rally during their stirring 34–31 overtime victory against the Miami Dolphins in their 1987 meeting in Joe Robbie Stadium?
   a) 14
   b) 17
   c) 21
   d) 28

●

6 What former Bills kicker once lamented: "Coaches treat us like cars. The old one is working fine, but they want a new one anyway. They think they'll enjoy it more."?
   a) Pete Gogolak
   b) Booth Lusteg
   c) Tom Dempsey
   d) John Leypoldt

●

BETTER LATE THAN NEVER

Fans and media tend to focus on a team's high draft choices, but often it is the middle- to late-round picks that spell the difference between being champs or chumps. The Bills have found some of their greatest players in the middle-to-late rounds. In fact, six members of their Silver Anniversary team were selected in the sixth round and beyond. Probably their most famous late pick was defensive tackle Tom Sestak, who was chosen out of McNeese State in the seventeenth round of the 1962 draft and went on to become one of the greatest players in American Football League history. Here's a look at some of the Bills' more productive middle-to-late-round draft picks.

1961   Al Bemiller, center, Syracuse, seventh round.
1962   Mike Stratton, linebacker, Tennessee, thirteenth round.
       Tom Sestak, defensive tackle, McNeese State, seventeenth round.
1963   George Saimes, defensive back, Michigan State, sixth round.
       Daryle Lamonica, quarterback, Notre Dame, twenty-fourth round.
1964   Pete Gogolak, kicker, Cornell, twelfth round.
       Hagood Clarke, defensive back, Florida, eighteenth round.
1971   Bobby Chandler, wide receiver, USC, seventh round.
1975   Roland Hooks, running back, North Carolina State, tenth round.
1976   Keith Moody, defensive back/kick returner, Syracuse, tenth round.
1977   Charles Romes, defensive back, North Carolina Central, twelfth round.
1978   Will Grant, center, Kentucky, tenth round.
1980   Greg Cater, punter, Tennessee-Chattanooga, tenth round.
1981   Robb Riddick, running back, Millersville (Pa.) State, ninth round.

AUTHOR'S NOTE: The Bills have made some good mid- to late-round selections in recent years. In time, players such as Jeff Wright (eighth round, '88), Carlton Bailey (ninth round, '88) and Howard Ballard (eleventh round, '87) may join the aforementioned on the Better-Late-Than-Never List.

The Bills drafted Tom Sestak, one of their all-time greats, in the seventeenth round of the 1962 draft. *(Buffalo Bills)*

7 In 1986, Bruce Smith set the unofficial club record for sacks. How many did he have?
   a) 12
   b) 13
   c) 14
   d) 15

●

8 What was the significance of the Bills' 27–20 victory against the Patriots on November 28, 1971?

●

9 Joe Cribbs had a sensational rookie year, rushing for 1,185 yards and catching 52 passes for 415 yards. But during that 1980 season, the running back also established an NFL record he wished he didn't possess. What was it?

●

10 In what year was the red standing buffalo on the Bills' helmets replaced by a modernistic, charging one?
   a) 1970   c) 1980
   b) 1974   d) 1984

●

11 Only three Bills receivers have surpassed 1,000 yards in a season. Who are they?

●

12 Name the current NFL head coach who once returned an interception 45 yards while playing linebacker for the Bills in 1967.

●

13 What Bills center once worked as a sheriff's deputy?
   a) Kent Hull
   b) Will Grant
   c) Mike Montler
   d) Al Bemiller

●

14 What wide receiver is Cookie Gilchrist's cousin?
   a) Elbert Dubenion
   b) Glenn Bass
   c) J. D. Hill
   d) Ahmad Rashad

●

15 Asked what the atmosphere on the Bills was like during their back-to-back 2–14 seasons in the mid-1980s, this player responded: "Remember Saigon in 1975 with everyone trying to get out?"

●

16 What Bills halfback was named AFL rookie of the year in 1966?

●

17 In which round was former Bills quarterback Joe Ferguson drafted?

●

18 From December 8, 1963, through November 15, 1964, the Bills set a club record for consecutive victories. How long was the winning streak?
   a) 10
   b) 11
   c) 12
   d) 13

●

19 True or false: Pete Gogolak has a better career field goal percentage than Scott Norwood.

●

20 What Bills punter was named after a comic musician?

●

21 Name the running back, who, in a 1971 game against Baltimore, was held to minus 10 yards in seven carries.

●

22 Who was the Bills' first general manager?
   a) Dick Gallagher
   b) Harvey Johnson
   c) Patrick McGroder
   d) Stew Barber

●

23 What "lucky" article of clothing did Ralph Wilson wear at each game during the Bills' 1988 season?

●

24 True or false: Tony Greene set an NFL record when he returned an interception 101 yards for a touchdown against Kansas City in 1976.

●

25 Who did the Bills trade to acquire Vince Ferragamo from the Los Angeles Rams in 1985?

●

26 During an October 11, 1964 game, Jack Kemp connected with this receiver for a 94-yard pass completion, longest in Bills history. Who was the receiver?
   a) Elbert Dubenion
   b) Glenn Bass
   c) Ernie Warlick
   d) Bo Roberson

●

27 What was Bruce Smith's nickname in college?

●

28 In 1987, this person joined the Bills payroll, becoming the first female scout in the National Football League. Who is she?

●

29 What former Bills linebacker is a high-ranking official in the NFL Players' Association?

●

30 Name the two head coaches who have served two tours of duty with the Bills.

●

31 What college jobs did Lou Saban take immediately after leaving the Bills in 1966 and 1976?

●

32 In a September 9, 1979 game, this Bills running back touched the ball only four times in the second half and scored each time.

●

33 This late Bills vice-president's son-in-law coaches in the National Basketball Association. Name the VP and the son-in-law.

●

34 True or false: The Bills have a winning record in overtime games.

●

35 Who holds the Bills record for most touchdowns in a single game?
  a) Cookie Gilchrist
  b) Jerry Butler
  c) O. J. Simpson
  d) Joe Cribbs

●

36 Who did O. J. Simpson get into a fight with, resulting in the Juice's only ejection of his NFL career?

●

37 What player gave up his job with the Washington Gas and Light company to become the Bills kicker?
  a) Booth Lusteg
  b) John Leypoldt
  c) Pete Gogolak
  d) Benny Ricardo

●

38 True or false: During the 1961 season, Patriots owner Billy Sullivan postponed a game against the Bills at Boston University for several days because of a hurricane warning.

●

39 What player was known as Marlin the Magician?

●

40 What cabinet position does Jack Kemp hold in the Bush Administration?

●

41 What former Bills quarterback played for Marv Levy at William and Mary College in the late 1960s?
  a) Dennis Shaw
  b) Dan Darragh
  c) Dan Manucci
  d) Gary Marangi

●

42 Who did the Bills part with to acquire Leonard Smith from the Phoenix Cardinals?

•

43 What defensive end avoids red meats and sleeps on the floor with his wife and five children?

•

44 What former Bills coach said: "I wouldn't build my offense around one back, no matter how good he is. It's too easy for the pros to set up defensive keys. O. J. can be a terrific pass receiver and we expect him to block, too."?

•

45 True or false: The Bills dropped a 1976 Thanksgiving game to Detroit, despite a 273-yard rushing performance by O. J. Simpson.

•

46 In 1988, Andre Reed led the team in receptions for the third straight season. Who was the last Bills receiver to top the Bills in catches for at least three years in a row?

   a) Bobby Chandler   c) Frank Lewis
   b) Jerry Butler   d) Ahmad Rashad

•

47 What Bills defender was Chiefs linebacker E. J. Holub talking about when he said: "Last week, he made a weenie outta Sweeney; today he made putty outta Budde."?

•

48 Name the Bills free agent defensive back who once dated Brooke Shields while the two were undergraduates at Princeton.

•

49 What coach and his players had to dodge a shower of beer cans—not all of them empty—during a 17–7 loss to the New York Titans at War Memorial Stadium on September 22, 1962?

   a) Harvey Johnson   c) Lou Saban
   b) Buster Ramsey   d) Joe Collier

•

50 What team did Marv Levy guide to two Canadian Football League titles?

Wide receiver Jerry Butler had a dynamic career cut short by injuries. *(Buffalo Bills)*

1. c) Billy Atkins. He also kicked 6-of-15 field goals for good measure.

2. True. The Bills used their No. 1 pick in 1979 to select Tom Cousineau. After failing to sign Cousineau, the Bills dealt the linebacker's rights to Cleveland in 1982 in exchange for the Browns' first pick in 1983. The Bills used that selection to draft Kelly.

3. Ralph Wilson.

4. O. J. Simpson. Late Bills equipment man Tony Marchitte had to contact Simpson's alma mater, Southern Cal, about obtaining the Juice's college headgear.

5. c) 21. Midway through the second quarter, the Bills trailed 21–0.

6. d) John Leypoldt.

7. d) 15.

8. It snapped a 15-game losing streak, longest in club history.

9. Cribbs set a league record for most fumbles by a running back with 16.

10. b) 1974.

11. Frank Lewis, 1,082 in 1979 and 1,244 in 1981; Marlin Briscoe, 1,036 in 1970; Elbert Dubenion, 1,139 in 1964.

12. Marty Schottenheimer.

13. c) Mike Montler.

14. a) Elbert Dubenion.

15. Fred Smerlas.

16. Bobby Burnett.

17. Third.

18. b) 11. The streak was halted by the Boston Patriots, 38–26 on November 15, 1964.

19. False. Norwood had a 75 percent accuracy rate (72 of 96) entering the 1988 season, while Gogolak made 63 percent of his kicks (47 of 75).

20. Spike Jones.

21. O. J. Simpson.

22. a) Dick Gallagher.

23. A rainbow-colored tie.

24. False. Greene's return was one yard shy of the NFL mark shared by four players.

25. Tony Hunter.

26. b) Glenn Bass.

27. The Sackman.

28. Linda Wilson Bogdan, Ralph Wilson's daughter.

29. Doug Allen.

30. Lou Saban and Harvey Johnson.

31. Following the 1965 season, Saban became head football coach at the University of Maryland. When he left during the 1976 season, he became athletic director at the University of Cincinnati, a job he held for 19 days.

32. Roland Hooks. After carrying just once for three yards (a non-scoring play) in the first half, Hooks scored on runs from the 3, 32, 4, and 28 after intermission as the Bills routed the Bengals, 51–24.

33. Patrick McGroder and John MacLeod.

34. True. The Bills are 6–2 in overtime games.

35. a) Cookie Gilchrist. He scored five touchdowns in a December 8, 1963 game vs. the New York Jets.

36. Mel Lunsford.

37. b) John Leypoldt.

38. True. Although some believe the real reason Sullivan pushed back the game for several days was because he didn't have the money to make payments.

39. Marlin Briscoe.

40. Director of Housing and Urban Development.

41. b) Dan Darragh.

42. Cornerback Roland Mitchell and a sixth-round draft pick that the Cardinals originally had sent to the Bills in exchange for Sean McNanie.

43. Art Still.

44. John Rauch.

45. True. The Juice's effort was in vain, as the Lions prevailed, 27–14.

46. a) Bobby Chandler, 1975–78.

47. Holub was talking about Bills defensive end Tom Sestak, who destroyed San Diego's Walt Sweeney and Kansas City's Ed Budde, two of the league's best offensive linemen.

48. Dean Cain.

49. c) Lou Saban.

50. Montreal Alouettes.

ABOUT THE AUTHOR

Scott Pitoniak has covered the Buffalo Bills for the Rochester (N.Y.) *Democrat and Chronicle* for the past five seasons. During that time, the magna cum laude graduate of Syracuse University has won several national and regional writing awards. His work has appeared in *Sport* magazine, *The Sporting News, USA Today,* the *Philadelphia Inquirer, Chicago Tribune,* and numerous other major magazines and newspapers. He also wrote a chapter in the book *College Football's 25 Greatest Teams,* published last fall by *The Sporting News.* He resides in Rochester with his wife, Susan, and their daughter, Amy.